Soldo

This book belongs to:

_____

About Ysolda

Ysolda Teague is a young Scottish designer who lives and works in Edinburgh. Her most recently published book is Little Red in the City, a guide to the perfect sweater and accompanying patterns. Travelling to promote it meant lots of time on the road and in the air that she spent developing these smaller projects that are ideal for fitting into busy lives.

Thank you!

to my mother, Sheena Stewart, and my assistants, Sarah Stanfield and Rebecca Redston, for taking care of everything else so that I can travel and work on new designs; to Julie Levesque for making the book so pretty, really getting it, and working as much as I do to meet deadlines; to all of the friends I've met through this wonderful knitting community who helped out by modelling, suggesting names and in so many, many other ways.

Text and illustrations copyright © 2011 Ysolda Teague

All photographs copyright © 2011 Ysolda Teague except:
Pages 49 & 54 - Ysolda wearing Roisin: Jessica Marshall Forbes

Printed and bound in America by Puritan Press on FSC® certified papers using vegetable based inks.
www.puritanpress.com

Whimsical Little Knits

by Golda

Confused?

Confused about something in one of the patterns, or have a question? The support page on my website contains links to useful resources, tutorials and frequently asked questions: **www.ysolda.com/support**

The patterns in this book have undergone extensive testing and technical editing to ensure that they're as error free as we can possibly make them. We are human, however, so if there any issues errata will be listed online at: **www.ysolda.com/wlk3/errata**

If you can't find the answer to your question or you think you might have found an error please email us at support@ysolda.com

INVISIBLE CAST ONS

A few of the patterns use specific cast on methods to give a neat, seamless beginning where stitches will be worked from both sides of the cast on simultaneously.

For the long cast on along the back of the hood on Roisin as well as the cast on at the beginning of Sherilyn the *figure-of-8* method is suggested, *Judy's magic cast on* can also be used.

Trinket and the Sherman socks both begin at the centre using an invisible circular cast on. There are several methods that can be used, I prefer the *disappearing-loop* method for its speed and simplicity but it can be tricky to work, the umbilical-cord method takes a little more time but is much easier.

Both the *figure-of-8* and *disappearing-loop* should be easy to find in good reference books and links to tutorials for all of these methods can be found online at: **www.ysolda.com/support/casting-on**

Abbreviations

beg - begin(ning)

bind off - aka cast off

C2B[k1tbl, k1] - sl1 st to cable needle and hold at front, k1tbl, k1 st from the cable needle

C2B[k1tbl, p1] - sl1 st to cable needle and hold at back, k1tbl, p1 st from the cable needle

C2F[k1, k1tbl] - sl1 st to cable needle and hold at front, k1, k1 st from the cable needle through the back loop

C2F[p1, k1tbl] - sl1 st to cable needle and hold at front, p1, k1 st from the cable needle through the back loop

C4B - slip 2 sts to cable needle and hold at back, k2, k2 sts from cable needle

C4F - slip 2 sts to cable needle and hold at front, k2, k2 sts from cable needle

CC - contrast colour

dec - decrease

dpn(s) - double pointed needle(s)

inc - increase

k - knit

k1tbl - knit through the back loop to produce a st that twists L

k2tog - knit 2 tog (a R leaning dec)

kfb - knit in the front and back of same st

m - stitch marker

m1 - make 1; work either as a m1L or m1R, used when the direction is not important and you can use the method you find easier, but be consistent

m1L - make one left - pick up the strand between the needles with L needle tip from the front and knit into the back of loop

m1p - make one purl - pick up the strand between the needles with L needle tip from the front and purl into back of loop

m1R - make one right - pick up the strand between the needles with the L needle tip from the back and knit it normally

MC - main colour

p - purl

p2tog - purl 2 together

patt - pattern

pfb - purl in the front and back of same st

pm - place marker

rem - remain(ing)

rep - repeat(ing)

rnd(s) - round(s)

RS - right side

sl - slip X st(s) - all sts are slipped one-by-one purlwise with yarn at WS unless otherwise stated

sl1, k2tog, psso - slip 1 st, knit 2 tog, lift slipped st over st just worked (a L leaning double dec)

sl1, k3tog, psso - slip 1 st, knit 3 tog, lift slipped st over st just worked (a L leaning triple dec)

sl2tog, k1, psso - slip 2 sts tog knitwise, k1, lift slipped sts over st just worked (a centered double dec)

slm - slip marker

ssk - slip, slip, knit - sl 2 sts knitwise individually, insert L needle into slipped sts from L to R, k these 2 sts tog (a L leaning dec)

st st - stockinette / stocking stitch

st(s) - stitch(es)

tk2tog - twisted k2tog - sl1 purlwise, insert needle into back of next st from back to front and slip, return both sts to L needle so that the 2nd one in from end is twisted, k these 2 sts tog (a R leaning twisted dec)

tog - together

tssk - twisted ssk - sl1 purlwise, sl1 knitwise, work these 2 sts tog as though doing a ssk (a L leaning twisted dec)

w+t - wrap and turn

WS - wrong side

wyib - with yarn in back

wyif - with yarn in front

yo - yarn over

yo2 - double yarn over

Oxidize

Oxidize features an asymmetrical cable panel that makes a basic ribbed beanie much more interesting to work, without sacrificing the things that make these beanies such a great classic. Truly my favourite kind of project, Oxidize is perfectly balanced between mindless and interesting, quick to complete, and easily adaptable to anyone's style.

Cables are worked with twisted slipped stitches that stand out very crisply from the background. Use either a single colour, or alternate two to give the effect of solid coloured cables against a subtly striped background (ignore references to CC and MC when working solid version). Varying the length and ease creates a fitted beanie or a loose, slouchy hat. The hat is completed with shaping worked neatly into the pattern, bringing the ribs and cable panel in to twine together at the top.

Materials

Yarn - worsted weight yarn in 1 or 2 colours (in equal amounts). Shown in A Verb For Keeping Warm Slick (75% superwash bfl wool, 25% silk, 240yds / 220m, 4oz / 113g) Solid version and CC for striped version - Indigo Blue Sky, MC for striped version - Supernova.

Short version - approx 110[130, 150, 170]yds / 100[120, 135, 155]m

Long version - approx 140[160, 180, 205]yds / 125[145, 165, 190]m

Needles - US 6 / 4mm 16" / 40cm circular and dpns or long circular(s) for preferred method of working small circumferences in the rnd.

Notions - stitch markers, cable needle.

Gauge

20 sts and 28 rnds = 4" / 10cm in twisted rib pattern.

Work swatch in the rnd in a basic twisted rib pattern:
even rnds: (p5, k1tbl, p2, k1tbl, p5);
odd rnds: (p5, sl1, p2, sl1, p5).

Sizes

Finished circumference of approx 17[19½, 22½, 25]" / 41[48, 55, 61]cm. For a loose, slouchier fit, work the size closest to actual head measurement. For a snug fit, work the size approximately 2" smaller than actual head measurement: for example, for a snug hat on a 22" head work the size 19½". Shown in short 19½" and long 22½".

Directions

With MC and 16″ / 40cm circular, cast on 84[98, 112, 126] sts and join rnd, pm to mark beg of rnd.

Rnd 1 - set up row: switch to CC, (p5, sl1, p2, sl1, p5) 2[3, 4, 5] times, pm to mark cable panel patt, p5, sl1, p2, *sl1, p4 rep from * 4 more times, sl1, p2, sl1, p5, pm to mark end of cable panel patt, p5, sl1, p2, sl1, p5.

WORKING THE HAT:

For two colour hat, use MC for even rounds and CC for odd rnds. Carry the unused yarn up the inside; don't break yarn after each rnd.

Work even rnds 2 - 66 from written directions or chart. When instructed to work in patt, work the sts as they appear, being careful to work knit sts through the back loop.

On all odd rnds: slip all sts that present as knits purlwise wyib and purl sts that present as purls.

Switch to dpns when stitches no longer fit comfortably on circular, about rnd 46.

COMPLETING THE HAT:

With MC: *tssk, rep from * to end, break yarn and draw through rem sts, pulling up tightly and securing tail on inside.

Weave in all ends and block.

Written directions

Rnds 2, 4, 6 & 8: (p5, k1tbl, p2, k1tbl, p5) 2[3, 4, 5] times, slm, p5, k1tbl, p2, *k1tbl, p4, rep from * 4 more times, k1tbl, p2, k1tbl, p5, slm, p5, k1tbl, p2, k1tbl, p5.

Rnd 3 and all following odd rnds: work in patt as described in directions for working the hat above.

Rnd 10: work in patt to m, slm, p5, k1tbl, *p2, C2F[p1, k1tbl], p2, C2B[k1tbl, p1], p2, rep from * twice more, k1tbl, p5, slm, work in patt to end.

Rnd 12: work in patt to m, slm, p5, k1tbl, *p3, C2F[p1, k1tbl], C2B[k1tbl, p1], p3, rep from * twice more, k1tbl, p5, slm, work in patt to end.

Rnd 14: work in patt to m, slm, p5, k1tbl, *p4, C2F[k1, k1tbl], p4, rep from * twice more, k1tbl, p5, slm, work in patt to end.

Rnd 16: work in patt to m, slm, p5, k1tbl, *p3, C2B[k1tbl, p1], C2F[p1, k1tbl], p3, rep from * twice more, k1tbl, p5, slm, work in patt to end.

Rnd 18: work in patt to m, slm, p5, k1tbl, *p2, C2B[k1tbl, p1], p2, C2F[p1, k1tbl], p2, rep from * twice more, k1tbl, p5, slm, work in patt to end.

Rnd 20: work in patt to m, slm, p5, (k1tbl, p2) twice, *p2, C2F[p1, k1tbl], p2, C2B[k1tbl, p1], p2, rep from * once more, (p2, k1tbl) twice, p5, slm, work in patt to end.

Rnd 22: work in patt to m, slm, p5, (k1tbl, p2) twice, *p3, C2F[p1, k1tbl], C2B[k1tbl, p1], p3, rep from * once more, (p2, k1tbl) twice, p5, slm, work in patt to end.

Rnd 24: work in patt to m, slm, p5, (k1tbl, p2) twice, *p4, C2B[k1tbl, k1], p4, rep from * once more, (p2, k1tbl) twice, p5, slm, work in patt to end.

Rnd 26: work in patt to m, slm, p5, (k1tbl, p2) twice, *p3, C2B[k1tbl, p1], C2F[p1, k1tbl], p3, rep from * once more, (p2, k1tbl) twice, p5, slm, work in patt to end.

Rnd 28: work in patt to m, slm, p5, (k1tbl, p2) twice, *p2, C2B[k1tbl, p1], p2, C2F[p1, k1tbl], p2, rep from * once more, (p2, k1tbl) twice, p5, slm, work in patt to end.

For longer version:
Repeat Rnds: 10 - 28 once more.

Rnd 30: work in patt to m, slm, p5, k1tbl, p2, (k1tbl, p4) twice, C2F[p1, k1tbl], p2, C2B[k1tbl, p1], (p4, k1tbl) twice, p2, k1tbl, p5, slm, work in patt to end.

Rnd 32: work in patt to m, slm, p5, k1tbl, p2, k1tbl, p4, k1tbl, p5, C2F[p1, k1tbl], C2B[k1tbl, p1], p5, k1tbl, p4, k1tbl, p2, k1tbl, p5, slm, work in patt to end.

Rnd 34: work in patt to m, slm, p5, k1tbl, p2, k1tbl, p4, k1tbl, p6, C2F[k1, k1tbl], p6, k1tbl, p4, k1tbl, p2, k1tbl, p5, slm, work in patt to end.

Rnd 36: work in patt to m, slm, p5, k1tbl, p2, k1tbl, p4, k1tbl, p5, C2B[k1tbl, p1], C2F[p1, k1tbl], p5, k1tbl, p4, k1tbl, p2, k1tbl, p5, slm, work in patt to end.

Rnd 38: *p4, C2B[k1tbl, p1], p2, C2F[p1, k1tbl], p4, rep from * 1[2, 3, 4] more times, slm, p4, C2B[k1tbl, p1], p2, (k1tbl, p4) twice, C2B[k1tbl, p1], p2, C2F[p1, k1tbl], (p4, k1tbl) twice, p2, C2F[p1, k1tbl], p4, slm, p4, C2B[k1tbl, p1], p2, C2F[p1, k1tbl], p4.

Rnd 40: *p3, C2B[k1tbl, p1], p4, C2F[p1, k1tbl], p3, rep from * 1[2, 3, 4] more times, slm, p3, C2B[k1tbl, p1], p3, (k1tbl, p4) 5 times, k1tbl, p3, C2F[p1, k1tbl], p3, slm, p3, C2B[k1tbl, p1], p4, C2F[p1, k1tbl], p3.

Rnd 42: (p2, tk2tog, p6, tssk, p2) 2[3, 4, 5] times, slm, p2, C2B[k1tbl, p1], p4, (k1tbl, p4) 6 times, C2F[p1, k1tbl], p2, slm, p2, tk2tog, p6, tssk, p2. 78[90, 102, 114] sts.

Rnd 44: (p1, tk2tog, p6, tssk, p1) 2[3, 4, 5] times, slm, p1, tk2tog, p5, *C2F[p1, k1tbl], p2, C2B[k1tbl, p1], p4, rep from * twice more, p1, tssk, p1, slm, p1, tk2tog, p6, tssk, p1. 70[80, 90, 100] sts.

(continued on page 15)

Chart Key

Q k1tbl

☐ p

Ϙ tk2tog

Ϩ tssk

▨ no stitch

⧖ C2B[k1tbl, k1]

⧗ C2F[k1, k1tbl]

⧖ C2B[k1tbl, p1]

⧗ C2F[p1, k1tbl]

☐ repeat the stitches inside this box

Chart Notes

a. basic ribbed panel - work a total of 2[3,4,5] times at beg of rnd

b. cable detail panel - work once for all sizes

c. rep basic ribbed 14 st panel once more at end of rnd

d. rep rows 10-28 once more for longer version

e. at the beg of rnd 48 and 62, remove m, sl 1, reposition m to mark new beginning of rnd, on following rnd stop 1 st from end and return m to this position

Chart - follow every row from right to left, refer to written direction for stitch counts after decrease rnds.

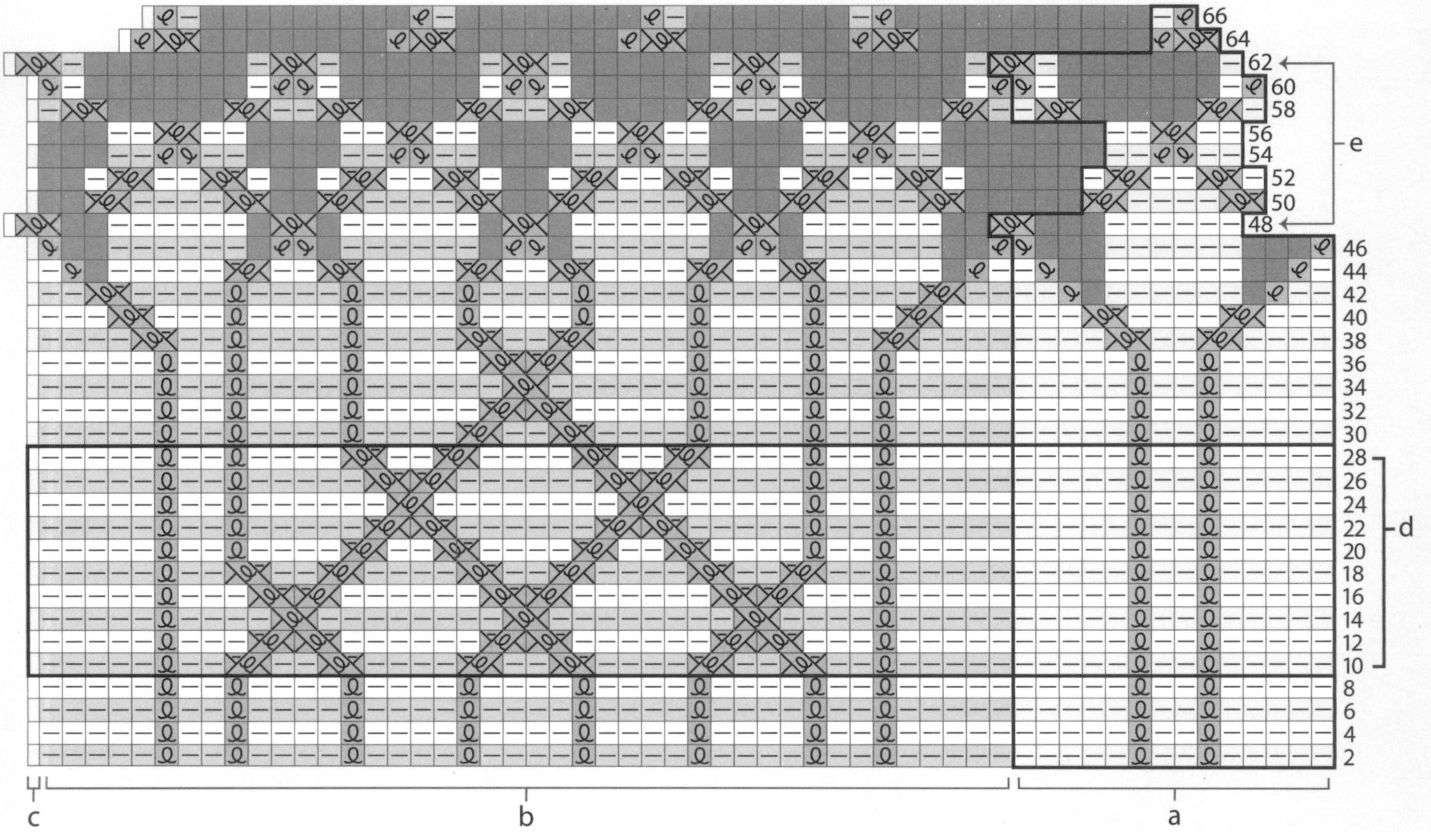

Oxidize

13

Oxidize would go perfectly with
the slipped stitches and stripes in
Stephen's Daybreak shawl pattern.

Rnd 46: (tk2tog, p6, tssk) to end, remove cable panel markers as you come to them. 56[64, 72, 80] sts.

Rnd 48: remove m, sl1, reposition m to mark new beginning of rnd, (p6, C2F[k1, k1tbl]) to end, on following rnd stop 1 st from end and return m to this position.

Rnd 50: (C2F[p1, k1tbl], p4, C2B[k1tbl, p1]) to end.

Rnd 52: (p1, C2F[p1, k1tbl], p2, C2B[k1tbl, p1], p1) to end.

Rnd 54: (p2, tssk, tk2tog, p2) to end. 42[48, 54, 60] sts.

Rnd 56: (p2, C2B[ktbl1, k1], p2) to end.

Rnd 58: (p1, C2B[k1tbl, p1], C2F[p1, k1tbl], p1) to end.

Rnd 60: (tk2tog, p2, tssk) to end. 28[32, 36, 40] sts.

Rnd 62: remove m, sl1, reposition m to mark new beginning of rnd (p2, C2F[k1, k1tbl]) to end, on following rnd stop 1 st from end and return m to this position.

Rnd 64: (C2F[p1, k1tbl], tk2tog) to end. 21[24, 27, 30] sts.

Rnd 66: (tk2tog, p1) to end. 14[16,18, 20] sts.

See page 10 for directions for completing the top of the hat.

Narwhal Mittens

Narwhals might seem mythically strange, and explorers once sold their tusks as "authentic unicorn horns", but they're real whales. They can be found inside the arctic circle and now they can keep your hands cosy in temperatures they'd be perfectly at home in. Traditional Selbuvotter mitten patterns on the cuffs and palms combine with fun details like the fish on the thumbs and, of course, the narwhals.

I love the fabric that the squishy, sport weight Chickadee gives in stranded colourwork at this range of gauges but heavier DK or worsted weight yarns such as Quince and Co. Lark could be used if you prefer your mittens to be very dense or wish to make them larger than the largest size given.

Materials

Yarn - Outer: sport weight yarn in 2 colours: 175[200, 215]yds / 160[185, 200]m MC and 100[110, 120] yds / 95[100, 110]m CC. Shown in Quince & Co. Chickadee (100% wool, 181yds / 166m, 1.76oz / 50g) in MC - Peacock and CC - Leek.

Lining: fingering / 4ply yarn: 200[215, 230]yds / 185[200, 215]m. Shown in Quince & Co. Tern (75% wool, 25% Silk, 221yds / 202m, 1.76oz / 50g) in Kelp.

Needles - US 2[2 ½, 3] / 2.75[3, 3.25]mm dpns or long circular(s) for preferred method of working small circumferences in the rnd.

US 4[5, 6] / 3.5[3.75, 4]mm dpns or long circular(s) for preferred method of working small circumferences in the rnd.

Notions - stitch markers, scrap yarn.

Gauge

15[14, 13]sts and 15[14, 13]rows = 2" / 5cm in stranded colour work in the rnd with larger needles.

Finished Sizes

Finished palm circumference of approx 8[8¾, 9¼]" / 20.5[22, 23.5] cm, choose a size with approx 1" / 2.5cm of positive ease.

Directions

PICOT HEM

With larger needle and scrap yarn provisionally cast on 48 sts. Join rnd, dividing sts evenly over needles. Switch to MC and k 7 rnds.

Next rnd: (k2tog, yo) to end.

K 7 rnds.

Undo provisional cast on and slip held sts onto smaller needle(s). Hold smaller needle behind working needle. Work 1 rnd by knitting each working st together with a cast on st, joining the sts and completing the hem. 48 sts on larger needle. Set smaller needles aside.

K 1 rnd.

CUFF

Join CC. Following charts for appropriate hand, and repeating charts to end of round, work chart A once, then chart B once, followed by chart A once more.

HAND

Arrange stitches for right mitt so that the first 30 sts are on needle 1 and 18 sts are on needle 2 or divided over needles 2 and 3. Arrange stitches for left mitt so that first 18 sts are on needle 1 or divided between needles 1 and 2 and 30 sts are on last needle.

K 2 rnds with MC.

Work main chart for the correct hand; referring to chart key for directions for creating thumbhole. 60 sts after thumb gusset increases have been worked, and 26 sts when chart is complete.

When chart is complete, arrange sts evenly on two needles so that 1 stitch from the 3-stitch side border is on the front at one side and 2 sts on the other. Kitchener stitch front sts to back using CC.

Chart A

Chart B

Charts, Right Mitten

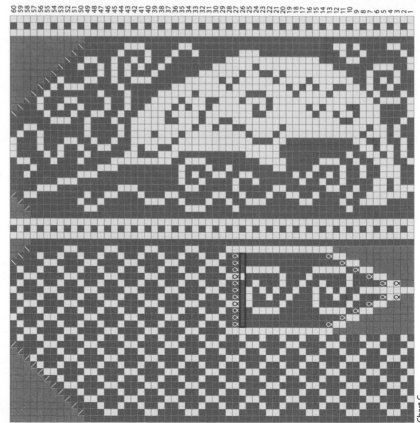

Chart C

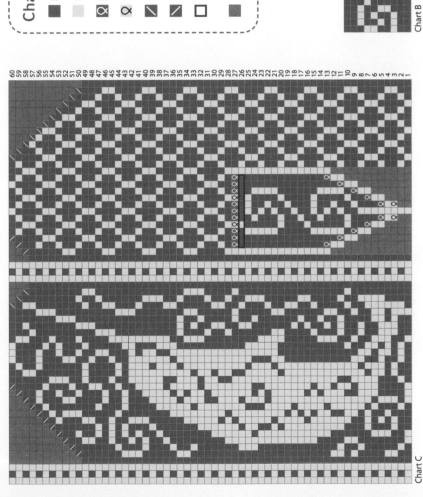

Chart A

Chart B

Charts, Left Mitten

Chart Key

■ k with MC
■ k with CC
⊠ backwards loop cast on 1 st with MC
⊘ backwards loop cast on 1 st with CC
◪ k2tog with MC
◪ ssk with MC
□ work as charted then slip all outlined sts just
worked to scrap yarn and continue round
■ no stitch

Chart C

Narwhal Mittens

19

Right thumb

Left thumb

Thumb

Return 11 held sts for thumb to larger needles. Join both MC and CC. Following rnd 1 of thumb chart, pick up and knit 13 sts (11 from the cast on stitches and 1 from each side). Continue across 11 held sts to complete rnd 1. 24 sts.

Join in the rnd and follow thumb chart until complete. Break yarn and draw MC through rem sts, fastening securely on the inside.

Lining

Turn mitten inside out. Using smaller needles and lining yarn, and starting at beginning of rnd, pick up and knit 1 st for each cast on st around inside of cuff along joining rnd of hem. 48 sts. Join rnd, dividing sts evenly over needles.

K 24 rnds.

Next rnd (right mitten): k13, pm, k to end.

Next rnd (left mitten): k34, pm, k to end.

Work thumb shaping for both hands the same way using m as set in previous rnd to place them correctly.

Next rnd: k to m, slm, m1, k1, m1, pm, k to end.

K 2 rnds.

Next rnd: k to m, slm, m1, k to m, m1, slm, k to end.

Rep last 3 rnds 4 more times. 13 thumb sts between markers.

K 18 rnds.

Next rnd: k to m, remove marker, slip next 13 thumb sts to scrap yarn, remove marker, cast on 11 using backwards loop cast on, k to end. 58 sts.

K 20 rnds, stopping 1 st from end of rnd on last rnd. This will be the new beginning of the rnd.

Even the best designers resort to store bought sweaters at times, but Melissa likes to incorporate a hand-knit accessory into her outfits.

Next rnd: ssk, k to 3 sts from end of rnd, k2tog, k1.

Next rnd: k.

Rep last 2 rnds 6 more times. 44 sts.

Next rnd: ssk, k17, k2tog, pm, k1, ssk, k to 3 sts from end of rnd, k2tog, k1.

Next rnd: k.

Next rnd: ssk, k to 2 sts from m, k2tog, slm, k1, ssk, k to 3 sts from end of rnd, k2tog, k1.

Repeat last 2 rnds twice more. 28 sts.

Divide sts over 2 needles and use kitchener st to close top of lining.

Thumb lining

Slip 13 held stitches for thumb onto smaller needles, join lining yarn and pick up and knit 12 stitches (10 from the cast on stitches and 1 from each side). 25 sts.

Next rnd: k1, k2tog, k10, ssk, k8, k2tog. 22 sts.

K 23 rnds.

Next rnd: (ssk, k6, k2tog, k1) twice. 18 sts.

K 1 rnd.

Next rnd: (ssk, k4, k2tog, k1) twice. 14 sts.

K 1 rnd.

Next rnd: (ssk, k2, k2tog, k1) twice. 10 sts.

Next rnd: (ssk, k2tog, k1) twice. 6 sts.

Break yarn and draw through rem sts, fastening securely on the inside.

Finishing

Bury any rem loose ends on inside between mitten and lining. Block. Turn lining to inside.

Not-so-tiny Slippers

One of my favourite patterns in the first Whimsical Little Knits is the Tiny Shoes, simple little baby Mary Janes with an I-cord strap. When the pattern came out, plenty of knitters seemed to like it just as much as I did, but some of them didn't just want to make tiny shoes. The question "could I make a pattern for Tiny Shoes for bigger feet" seemed to have an obvious answer: "no, the proportions are all wrong, they'll be much too wide and short." But, I'm nothing if not contrary, and once I'd decided that scaling up the Tiny Shoes pattern wouldn't work, it proved impossible to completely let go of the idea.

Two books later, although it was included as a possibility in the first outline of Whimsical Little Knits 2, it had percolated for long enough. The answer to the proportions issue is, as the answer to more interesting shapes in knitting so often is, short rows. In fact these would be an excellent project on which to try out the technique for the first time. It's hard to compete with the cuteness of baby toes wrapped in wool, but a lot of trial and error resulted in visual proportions that come as close as possible. The stitches themselves are scaled up, the chunky gauge makes for a project that can be completely almost as quickly as the tiny version and there are few things as wonderfully cozy as walking around the house on a thick bed of garter stitch. For slippery floors it may be a good idea to add non-stick paint or iron-on pads.

Materials

Yarn - bulky weight yarn: 95yds / 85m. Shown in O-Wool Legacy Bulky (100% certified organic merino, 106yds / 97m, 3.53oz / 100g) in 2050 Lava.

Needles - US 10 / 6mm 16" / 40cm circular.

Notions - stitch markers, 2 1" / 2.5cm buttons.

Gauge

13 sts and 19 rows = 4" / 10cm in st st.

Sizes

To fit foot length of approx 8½[9½, 10½]" / 21.5[24, 26.5]cm. Slippers will stretch to fit.

Strap

Make 2.

Cast on 4 sts, work I-cord as follows: *k4, slide sts to other end of needle without turning, rep from *, for 54[58, 62]rows, bind off 2 sts, continue in I-cord on rem 2 sts for 8 more rows, bind off.

Left slipper

Beginning at cast-on end of strap, pick up and knit 44[48, 52]sts along I-cord, picking up 1 st for every row, working into the slightly loose strand between the first and last sts along the back, remaining I-cord will form strap across foot.

Cable cast on 9 sts next to last picked up st and join rnd. 53[57, 61]sts. K 22[24, 26]sts, pm - this will now mark the beginning of the rnd. K 1 rnd.

Continue below at "Both slippers".

Right slipper

Beginning at cast-on end of strap, pick up and purl 44[48, 52]sts, picking up sts from strands of yarn across back of I-cord, cable cast on 9 sts next to last picked up stitch. Turn work and knit across all sts, join rnd. 53[57, 61]sts; K31[33, 35]sts, pm - this will now mark the beginning of the rnd.

Both slippers

Next rnd: k25[27, 29], (yo, k1) 4 times, k to end. 57[61, 65]sts.

Next rnd: k.

HEEL SHORT ROWS

Next row: k9[10, 11], w+t.

Next row: p to m, slm, p9[10, 11]w+t.

Next row: k to m, slm, k5[7, 9], w+t.

Next row: p to m, slm, p5[7, 9], w+t.

TOE SHORT ROWS

Next row: k to m, slm, k38[41, 44] picking up wraps and knitting them tog with wrapped sts, w+t.

Next row: p19[21, 23], w+t.

Next row: k5[6, 7], (m1, k3) 3 times, m1, k3[4, 5], w+t. 61[65, 69]sts.

Next row: p19[21, 23], w+t.

Next row: k17[19, 21], w+t.

Next row: p15[17, 19], w+t.

Next row: k13[15, 17], w+t.

Next row: p11[13, 15], w+t.

Next row: k9[11, 13], w+t.

Next row: p7[9, 11]w+t.

Next row: k5[7, 9], w+t.

Next row: p3[5, 7], w+t.

Next row: k to m, picking up wraps and knitting them tog with wrapped sts.

SOLE

Beg with a k rnd, work 4 rnds in garter st; on first rnd pick up wraps and knit them tog with wrapped sts.

Next rnd: k3, k2tog, k20[22, 24], ssk, k7, k2tog, k to 5 sts from end of rnd, ssk, k3. 57[61, 65]sts.

Next rnd: p.

Next rnd: k2, k2tog, k20[22, 24], ssk, k5, k2tog, k to 4 sts from end of rnd, ssk, k2. 53[57, 61]sts.

Next rnd: p.

Next rnd: k1, k2tog, k20[22, 24], ssk, k3, k2tog, k7, w+t.

Next row: k19, w+t.

Next row: k7, ssk, k1, k2tog, k to 3 sts from end of rnd, picking up wraps and knitting them tog with wrapped sts, ssk, k1.

Next rnd: p.

Finishing

Kitchener st from heel to toe, bringing yarn through last odd stitch at toe and drawing through to the inside.

Sew narrow section of strap into a loop, joining the two bound-off edges. Sew button securely to cast-on end of strap.

Trinket

This little robot has all of the most important features: wheels for speeding around on adventures, dials and gauges, an antenna for communicating important messages (or chewing on), long arms for reaching everything and a pocket for carrying your most treasured toys and trinkets. The body, head and antenna are worked in the round in one piece and stitches for the arms and wheels are picked up from the stuffed body. The pocket is actually a solution to a technical problem, I didn't want to deal with working the intarsia panels on the front in the round, but nor did I want a seam: the pocket panel neatly fills the space.

Materials

Yarn - chunky / heavy aran weight yarn in 2 colours: approx 150yds /140m of each colour. Shown in Quince & Co. Osprey (100% wool, 170yds /155m, 3.53oz /100g) in MC - Bird's Egg and CC - Carrie's Yellow.

Needles - US 7 /4.5mm 16" /40cm circular and dpns or long circular(s) for preferred method of working small circumferences in the rnd.

Notions - stitch markers, toy stuffing (eg. polyfill or wool).

Gauge

17 sts and 26 rnds = 4" /10cm in st st in the rnd. Because the finished size isn't important different yarn weights can be used. Use a needle 2-3 sizes smaller than the suggested needle for that yarn to obtain a tight gauge that won't allow stuffing to show through.

Sizes

Approx 10" /25cm tall, not including antenna.

Notes

When working on dpns, magic loop or 2 circulars the pattern is written with markers as reference points for shaping, but some of these reference points can be marked with a divide in the sts between needles if preferred. Which reference points will be marked in this way depends on the method chosen for working small circumferences in the rnd so they aren't specified.

Before beginning wind off a small ball or bobbin of MC (approx 8yds / 7.5m) that will be used to work the intarsia front panels.

Body and head

Worked as one piece.

BASE

Using invisible circular method (see p.4), cast on 8 sts in MC. Divide sts evenly onto needles for preferred method of working small circumferences in the rnd.

Rnds 1, 3, 5, 7, 9, 11 and 13: k.

Rnd 2: kfb to end. 16 sts.

Rnd 4: (kfb, k6, kfb) twice. 20 sts.

Rnd 6: (kfb, pm, kfb, k5, kfb, pm, kfb, k1) twice. 28 sts.

Rnds 8, 10, 12, 14: (k to 1 st before m, kfb, slm, kfb) 4 times, k to end. 36, 44, 52, 60 sts.

STRIPED BUMPER

Switch to short circular needle; carry colour not in use up inside without breaking between stripes.

K 1 rnd, removing markers as you come to them.

CC stripe: k 1 rnd, p3 rnds.

MC stripe: k3 rnds, p3 rnds, k2 rnds.

Work CC stripe once more; don't break CC yarn.

Switch to MC and k 3 rnds.

SECTION WITH FRONT PANELS AND SPACE FOR BACK POCKET

The front panels are worked in intarsia, a space for the back pocket panel is bound off at the centre back which allows the section to be worked back and forth - making the intarsia panels much simpler to work. Make sure to twist the yarns together when changing colours.

Next rnd: with MC, k6, pm, k18, pm, k14, bind off 14, k to end of rnd.

29

Front panels chart

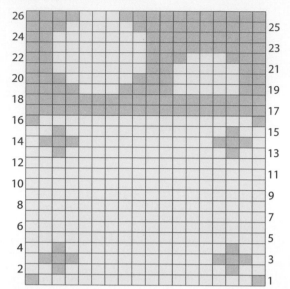

Features chart

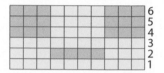

Right now Ellie is most interested in chewing on Trinket's antenna.

Next row: k to m in MC, slm, loosely carrying CC up inside of work and joining small ball of MC as required, work sts between markers from front panels chart, slm, k to bound off sts, turn.

Beginning with a purl row, work 25 rows in st st, working sts between markers from front panels chart and sts on either side in MC.

Next row (RS): with MC knit to gap, don't turn, cast on 14 sts, rejoin rnd. K8, pm to mark beg of rnd. Break extra yarns.

HEAD
K 2 rnds in MC, break yarn.

Switch to CC and k 19 rnds.

Next rnd: (k10, pm) to end.

Dec rnd: (k to 2 sts before m, k2tog, slm) to end. 54 sts.

K 1 rnd; work dec rnd once more; k 1 rnd; work dec rnd 7 more times. 6 sts rem.

Next rnd: (k1, k2tog) twice. 4 sts.

ANTENNA
Switch to MC and slip all 4 sts onto a single dpn (or the short circular needle). Work 2½″ / 7cm of I-cord as follows: *k4, slide sts to other end of needle without turning, rep from *. Break yarn leaving a 12″ / 30cm tail.

Next row: switch to CC, kfb to end. 8 sts.

Divide sts evenly onto needles for preferred method of working small circumferences in the rnd.

K 4 rnds with CC.

Next rnd: k2tog to end. Break yarn and draw through remaining 4 sts. Stuff ball on end of antenna with a small amount of stuffing. Pull yarn up tightly and thread back through I-cord to inside of head.

Thread MC down through I-cord, bringing it out ¼ of the way down. Fold I-cord and make a small stitch to hold the fold in place. Repeat this process on the other side of I-cord, lower down. Bring all rem tails through I-cord to inside of head and tie off ends in pairs.

Embroidering features
Positioning mouth on the fifth row of CC above the body, and making sure to centre features, duplicate stitch eyes and mouth in MC following features chart.

Chain stitch "needles" on dials in MC.

Back panel with pocket

Knit in the round from sts picked up around the hole in the back of the body.

Use MC and needles for preferred method of working small circumferences in the rnd. Beg at bottom right corner pick up and knit 14 sts along bound-off sts across bottom of hole, pm, 18 sts up left side, pm, 14 sts across top, pm, and 18 sts down right side. Join rnd, pm to mark beg of rnd.

Switch to CC without breaking MC, k 1 rnd, p 3 rnds. Switch to MC, k 1 rnd.

Next rnd: *ssk, k to 2 sts before marker, k2tog, slm, k1, ssk, k to 3 sts before marker, k2tog, k1, slm, rep from * once more.

Rep last 2 rnds once more. 10 sts at bottom and top, 14 sts on each side.

FRONT OF POCKET

Worked in rows, decreasing with sts adjacent to "flap" to join sides.

Switch to CC and k to 1 st before marker, ssk, removing marker after slipping first st. Turn. Leave sts not being worked on needles, arranged so that the sts from the top of the pocket are resting on a dpn or cable of circular and the sts at the side are on the "active" needles, on either side of the sts in CC being worked.

Next row (WS): sl1, p to 1 st before marker, sl1, remove marker, return slipped st to left needle and p2tog. Turn.

Next row: sl1, k to slipped st, ssk (using one CC st and one MC st). Turn.

Next row: sl1, p to slipped st, p2tog (using one CC st and one MC st). Turn.

Rep last 2 rows 10 more times. 14 sts in MC rem.

Tie off loose ends from beg of pocket on inside. Stuff the body as much as possible without making working the sts on the needles too awkward.

INSIDE OF POCKET

K10, switch to MC and k across all rem sts including those left at the top. Join rnd. 24 sts.

Break CC and k 16 more rnds in MC.

Arrange sts so that there are 12 from the front and 12 from the back on each of 2 needles. Finish stuffing the body. Use a 3rd needle to join base of pocket with a three-needle-bind-off.

Bury rem ends on inside and push pocket to inside.

Wheels

Make 2 the same.

Picked up from sides of body and worked in the rnd.

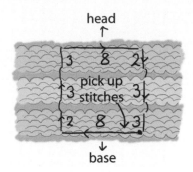

Use MC and needles for preferred method of working small circumferences in the rnd. Beg on first row of lowest CC stripe on body, and centering wheel between front and back, pick up and k8 sts on each side around a square. Pick up all sts from purl sts of stripes. Join rnd, pm to mark beg of rnd. 32 sts.

K 2 rnds.

Next rnd: (kfb, k3) to end. 40 sts.

Switch to CC. K 1 rnd, p 7 rnds.

Switch to MC. K 2 rnds.

Next rnd: (k3, k2tog) to end. 32 sts.

Next rnd: (k2, k2tog) to end. 24 sts.

Next rnd: (k1, k2tog) to end. 16 sts.

Tie off loose ends on inside and stuff.

Next rnd: k2tog to end. Break yarn and draw through remaining sts, going around twice, pull up tightly and bury tail on inside.

Arms

Make 2 the same.

Picked up from sides of body and worked in the rnd.

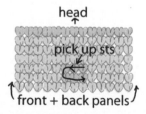

head

pick up sts

front + back panels

Count 4 rows down from top of body MC section. With MC and needles for preferred method of working small circumferences in the rnd pick up and knit centre 3 sts between front and back panels. Turn and pick up 3 more sts across the row immediately below.

Join rnd and k 6 rnds. Switch to CC, breaking MC.

Next rnd: (k2, kfb) twice. 8 sts.
*P 3 rnds, k 3 rnds; rep from * 5 more times. P 3 rnds.

HAND
Switch to MC, breaking CC. K 4 rnds.

Next rnd: k1, (m1, k2) 3 times, m1, k1. 12 sts.

K 1 rnd.

Next rnd: (k1, m1, k4, m1, k1) twice. 16 sts.

K 1 rnd.

Next rnd: k9, k2tog, k2, ssk, k1. 14 sts.

Next rnd: k8, k2tog, k2, ssk. 12 sts.

K 2 rnds.

Next rnd: ssk, k4, k2tog, k4. 10 sts.

K 1 rnd.

Next rnd: ssk, k2, k2tog, k4. 8 sts.

Stuff hand, leaving arm unstuffed. Divide sts for front and back of hand over 2 needles and kitchener stitch together.

Vintage Button Gloves

Long, elegant gloves with a simple twisted stitch cable pattern that follows the taper of the wrist. Closely spaced buttons down the outside of each cuff are inspired by vintage kid gloves, but since knitting is so much stretchier this version is much more practical. The buttons are purely decorative, no fussing with making buttonholes *or* fastening so many. It's the perfect opportunity to use delicate mother of pearl buttons, try using mismatched ones for a slightly quirky effect if you don't have a set of twenty four. Big bags of random mother of pearl buttons are among the many things I find almost impossible to resist in antique shops.

The Vintage Button Gloves pattern was first published in St-Denis Magazine Fall/Winter 2009, and the St-Denis yarn was too perfectly vintage in style to change it.

Materials

Yarn - dk weight yarn: approx 250[300]yds / 230[275]m. Shown in St-Denis Nordique (100% wool, 150yd / 137m, 1.76oz / 50g) in Eggplant.

Needles - US 4 / 3.5mm dpns or long circular(s) for preferred method of working small circumferences in the rnd.

Notions - stitch markers, cable needle, scrap yarn, 24 ⅜″/10mm buttons. Buttons are decorative and do not need to fit buttonholes so the size required is flexible.

Gauge

24 sts and 32 rnds = 4″/10cm in reverse st st in the rnd.

Sizes

Palm circumference of 7¼[8¾]″ / 18.5[22]cm. Cuff approx 8″ / 20.5cm[8¼″ / 21cm] long. Choose size closest to actual measurement or with slight positive ease. Shown in larger size.

Baby Carson keeps Sarah pretty cozy so long gloves are perfect for keeping just her chilly hands warm.

Stitch Guide

RIGHT CABLE

Rnds 1-3: k1tbl, p2, k1tbl.

Rnd 4: C2F[p1, k1tbl], C2B[k1tbl, p1].

Rnd 5: p1, C2F[k1, k1tbl], p1.

Rnd 6: C2B[k1tbl, p1], C2F[p1, k1tbl].

Rep rnds 1-6 for pattern.

LEFT CABLE

Rnds 1-3: k1tbl, p2, k1tbl.

Rnd 4: C2F[p1, k1tbl], C2B[k1tbl, p1].

Rnd 5: p1, C2B[k1tbl, k1], p1.

Rnd 6: C2B[k1tbl, p1], C2F[p1, k1tbl].

Rep rnds 1-6 for pattern.

CABLE END SEQUENCE

Rnd 1: C2B[k1tbl, p1], p2, C2F[p1, k1tbl].

Rnd 2: k1tbl, p4, k1tbl.

Rep rnd 2 for pattern.

Cable Charts

Right cable

Left cable

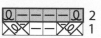

Cable end sequence

Chart Key

Ⓠ	k1tbl
⊟	p
⧄	C2B[k1tbl, k1]
⧅	C2F[k1, k1tbl]
⧄	C2B[k1tbl, p1]
⧅	C2F[p1, k1tbl]
☐	repeat the stitches inside this box

Right Glove

CUFF

Cast on 54[62]sts and join rnd, arranging sts in 3 sections as described below for your preferred working method with 19[22]sts in section 1, 16[18]sts in section 2 and 19[22]sts in section 3.

For dpns: arrange sts so that each section is on 1 of 3 needles.

For magic loop or 2 circulars: arrange sts so that sections 1 and 3 are on one half or needle with the beg of the rnd marked and section 2 is on the other half or needle.

Set up rnd: p11[13]sts, k3, p5[6]sts, k1tbl, p5[6]sts, pm, work rnd 1 of Right Cable patt, pm p5[6]sts, k1tbl, p to end.

Work 14[17]rnds in patt, repeating rnds 1-6 of Right Cable patt over 4 sts between markers.

*Dec rnd: p2tog, work in patt to 2 sts before first m, p2tog, slm, work Right Cable patt, slm, p2tog, work in patt to last 3 sts, p2tog, p1. 50[58]sts.

Work 11 rnds in patt.

Rep from * 3 more times. 38[46]sts.

THUMB GUSSET

Before starting thumb increases rearrange sts by slipping first 4[5]sts from section 3 to section 2. Sts are now arranged with 15[18], 12[15], 11[13] sts in each section.

Set-up Increases (Hand and Thumb): p15[18] (faux button band sts will be purled from now on), k1tbl, p1[2], m1p, slm, work Right Cable chart, slm, m1p, p1[2], k1tbl, p4[5], pm for thumb, m1p, p2, m1p, pm for thumb, p9[11]. 42[50]sts.

Work 2 rnds in patt.

Inc Rnd 1 (Thumb only): work in patt to first thumb m, slm, m1p, p to second thumb m, m1p, slm, p to end. 44[52]sts.

Work 2 rnds in patt.

Rep the last 3 rnds twice more. 48[56]sts.

Inc Rnd 2 (Hand and Thumb): work in patt to first cable m, m1p, slm, work Right Cable patt, slm, m1p, work in patt to first thumb m, slm, m1p, p to second thumb m, m1p, slm, p to end. 52[60]sts.

Work 2 rnds in patt.

Rep Inc Rnd 1. 54[62]sts.

Work 2 rnds in patt.

Repeat the last 3 rnds 2[3] more times, ending with rnd 3 of Right Cable patt. 58[68]sts.

Next rnd: p to 1 st before first cable m, pm, work rnd 1 of Cable End Sequence over next 6 sts (removing m), pm, p to first thumb m, place next 18[20]sts on scrap yarn for thumb, remove thumb markers. Cast on 4 sts, p to end. 44[52]sts.

Next 3 rnds: p to first m, work rnd 2 of Cable End Sequence, p to end. P 4[6]rnds.

PINKIE

P 14[16], place next 34[40]sts on scrap yarn (this will include some sts beyond the end of rnd). 10[12]sts remain.

Cast on 4 sts over gap, divide appropriately among needles, pm and join rnd. 14[16]sts.

P 16[20]rnds or until pinkie measures ¼" / 0.5cm less than desired length.

Dec rnd: (p1, p2tog) to last 2[1]sts, p2[1]. 10[11]sts.

Next rnd: p.

Dec rnd: (p2tog) 5 times, p0[1]. 5[6] sts. Break yarn leaving long tail and draw through remaining sts.

HAND

Transfer all held hand sts onto needles, rejoin yarn, mark beginning of rnd, and pick up and purl 4 sts from pinkie cast-on sts. Arrange these 38[44]sts evenly over needles and purl 4 rnds.

RING FINGER

P4 picked up sts, p5[6]sts across back of hand, transfer next 24[28]sts to scrap yarn. Cast on 4 sts over gap, p5[6] rem sts, pm and join rnd. 18[20]sts.

P 18[22]rnds or until finger measures ¼" / 0.5 cm less than desired length.

Dec rnd: (p1, p2tog) to last 0[2]sts, p0[2]. 12[14]sts.

Next rnd: p.

Dec rnd: p2tog 6[7] times. Break yarn leaving long tail and draw through remaining sts.

MIDDLE FINGER

Transfer 5[6]sts from each side of scrap yarn next to ring finger to needle. Rejoin yarn and p across palm sts, pick up and p 4 sts from ring finger cast-on sts, p across back-of-hand sts, cast on 4 sts over gap, pm and join rnd. 18[20]sts.

P 22[26]rnds or until finger measures ¼" / 0.5 cm less than desired length.

Shape top of finger and fasten off as for ring finger.

INDEX FINGER

Transfer 14[16]sts rem held sts onto needles. Rejoin yarn and pick up and p 4 sts from middle finger cast-on sts, pm and join rnd. 18[20]sts.

P 18[22]rnds or until finger measures ¼" / 0.5 cm less than desired length.

Shape top of finger and fasten off as for ring finger.

THUMB

Transfer 18[20] held thumb sts to needles. Rejoin yarn and pick up and p 4 sts from hand cast-on sts, pm and join rnd. 22[24]sts.

P 18[22]rnds or until thumb measures 1/4″ / 0.5 cm less than desired length.

Dec rnd: (p1, p2tog) to last 1[0]sts, p1[0]. 15[16]sts.

Next rnd: p.

Dec rnd: p2tog 7[8]times, p1[0].

Break yarn leaving long tail and draw through remaining sts.

Left glove

CUFF

Cast on and arrange sts on needles as for Right Glove.

Set up rnd: p19[22], k1tbl, p5[6], work rnd 1 of Left Cable patt over next 4 sts, pm, p5[6], k1tbl, p5[6], k3, p to end.

Work 14[17]rnds in patt, rep rnds 1-6 of Left Cable patt over 4 sts between markers.

*Dec rnd: p1, p2tog, work in patt to 2 sts before first m, p2tog, work Left Cable patt, slm, p2tog, work in patt to last 2 sts, p2tog. 50[58]sts.

Work 11 rnds in patt.

Rep from * 3 more times. 38[46]sts.

THUMB GUSSET

Before starting thumb increases rearrange sts by slipping last 4[5]sts from section 1 to section 2. Sts are now arranged with 11[13], 12[15], 15[18] sts in each section.

Set-up Increases (Hand and Thumb): p9[11], pm for thumb, m1p, p2, m1p, pm for thumb, p4[5], k1tbl, p1[2], m1p, slm, work Left Cable patt, slm, m1p, p1[2], k1tbl, p15[18] (faux button band sts will be purled from now on). 42[50]sts

Work 2 rnds in patt.

Inc Rnd 1 (Thumb only): work in patt to first thumb m, slm, m1p, p to second thumb m, m1p, slm, p to end. 44[52]sts.

Work 2 rnds in patt.

Rep the last 3 rnds twice more. 48[56]sts.

Inc Rnd 2 (Hand and Thumb): work in patt to first thumb m, m1p, slm, p to second thumb m, m1p, slm, work in patt to first cable m, m1p, slm, work Left Cable patt, slm, m1p, work in patt to end. 52[60]sts.

Work 2 rnds in patt.

Rep Inc Rnd 1. 54[62]sts.

Work 2 rnds in patt.

Repeat the last 3 rnds 2[3] more times, ending with rnd 3 of Right Cable patt. 58[68]sts

Next rnd: p to first thumb m, place next 18[20]sts on scrap yarn for thumb, remove thumb markers. Cast on 4 sts, p to 1 st before first cable m, pm, work rnd 1 of Cable End Sequence over next 6 sts (removing m), pm, p to end. 44[52]sts.

Next 3 rnds: p to first m, work rnd 2 of Cable End Sequence over next 6 sts, p to end.

P 4[6]rnds.

PINKIE

P 40[46], transfer next 34[40]sts to scrap yarn (this will include some sts beyond the end of rnd). 10[12]sts remain. Cast on 4 sts over gap, pm and join in rnd. 14[16]sts.

Complete as for right glove, reversing terms for palm and back of hand.

Finishing

Weave in all ends securely on inside, block. Sew 12 buttons evenly spaced down each faux button band.

Hendreary

Celebrate your love for buttons with this hat featuring giant ones in stranded colourwork. The buttons are worked against a traditional "lice" pattern, which, despite the gross name, is an excellent way to work a non-repeating motif in stranded colourwork. The allover pattern allows both colours to be used all the way around the hat, making the knitting simple and the hat cosier with the resulting double thick layer. There are a few sections in the large blocks of contrast colour on the buttons where you will need to twist the two yarns together in order to avoid long floats. Pay attention to colour dominance, for the buttons to stand out well against the patterned background make sure that the contrast colour is dominant.

Achieving the right balance of simple but recognisable buttons took some trial and error: the first version ended up as more of a cookie hat. The soft, luxurious yak and cormo blend held up delightfully well to all of that ripping and re-knitting and is one of the warmest yarns I've used. A slight halo gives the colourwork softly rounded edges that makes a big difference to whether the pattern reads as buttons.

Materials

Yarn - worsted weight yarn in 2 colours: MC 120yds / 110m, CC 70yds / 65m. Shown in Bijou Basin Ranch Bijou Bliss (50% Yak, 50% Cormo wool, 150yds / 137m, |1.98oz / 56g) in MC - Steel and CC - Goldenrod.

Needles - US 6 / 4mm 16″ / 40cm circular.

US 7 / 4.5mm 16″ / 40cm circular and dpns or long circular(s) for preferred method of working small circumferences in the rnd.

Notions - stitch markers, balloon for blocking.

Gauge

18 sts and 28 rnds = 4″ / 10cm in st st in the rnd with larger needles.

24 sts and 24 rnds = 4″ / 10cm in stranded colour work in the rnd with larger needles.

Sizes

s[m, l] to fit head circumference of approx 19[21, 24]″ / 48[53, 61]cm - fit as shown is loose and slouchy.

Directions

RIBBING

With smaller needle and MC, cast on 92[104, 116]sts. For best results use a tubular cast-on for (k2, p2) rib.

Work 16 rnds in (k2, p2) rib.

Switch to larger circular needle.

Next rnd: (sl2, k2) around, slipping the k sts and knitting the p sts.

BUTTON SECTION

Next rnd: k12[8, 4], (k3, kfb) to end. 112[128, 144]sts.

Next rnd: k20[28, 36], pm, k56, pm, k to end.

Next 36 rnds: work in lice patt to m, slm, work button chart to m, slm, work in lice patt to end.

CROWN SHAPING

Next 2 rnds: work in lice patt to end, removing markers as you come to them on first rnd.

Next 12 rnds: work crown shaping chart 7[8, 9] times around. 98[112, 126]; 84[96, 108]; 70[80, 90]; 56[64, 72]; 42[48, 54]; 28[32, 36]; 14[16, 18]; 7[8, 9]sts after each decrease rnd.

Break yarns and draw CC through rem sts, pulling up tightly and fastening on inside.

Finishing

Weave in ends and block. Blocking over an inflated balloon works well.

Button chart - follow every row from right to left

Chart Key

- ◼ k with MC
- ◼ k with CC
- ◪ sl2tog, k1, psso with CC
- ◩ k2tog with CC
- ◼ no stitch
- ☐ repeat the stitches inside this box

Lice pattern chart

Crown shaping chart

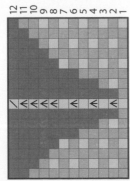

47

Roisin

A sweet pixie hood inspired both by cute patterns from the forties for little girls and more glamorous ones of starlets in headscarves. The vintage patterns I looked at involved working separate rectangles for hood and scarf, but this one uses a neat cast on method more commonly used for toe up socks to begin the hood and scarf together at the centre back. The scarf is biased which causes it to flare outward at the back neck, gives definition to the hood, and creates pointed ends. All of the stitch patterns used are variations on the same simple but effective technique where slipping stitches leaves strands of yarn across the right side that are later picked up.

Materials

Yarn - fingering weight yarn: 380yds / 350m.

Blue version shown in Alisha Goes Around Tiding of Magpies Fingering (63% merino, 20% silk, 15% nylon, 2% silver; 400yd / 366m, 3.49oz / 99g) in Mist.

Cream version shown in Excelana 4 ply Luxury Wool (100% pure new British Wool, 174yds / 159m, 1.76oz / 50g) in Natural Alabaster.

Needles - US 5 / 3.75mm 24" / 60cm or longer circular.

Notions - stitch markers, stitch holders.

Gauge

22 sts and 28 rows = 4" / 10cm in st st.

Finished Sizes

s[m, l]: 9[9¾, 10½]" / 22.75[24.75, 26.5]cm centre back to edge of hood, 11[12, 13]" / 28[30.5, 33]cm top of hood to neck, 3½" / 9cm scarf width, 40(41, 42)" / 101.5[104.25, 106.75] cm scarf length.

Stitch Guide

ARROW EDGING
(worked over 5 sts)

Row 1 (RS): sl5 wyif.

Row 2: sl5 wyib.

Rows 3 and 4: k.

Row 5: k2, pick up loose strands from front with L needle and k them tog with next st, k2.

Row 6: k2, sl1 wyif, k2.

Rep rows 1 - 6 for pattern.

SCATTERED ARROWS
(multiple of 12 sts + 1)

Rows 1-6: work in st st, beg with a k row.

Row 7 (RS): k4, *sl5 wyif, k7, rep from * to 9 sts from end, sl5 wyif, k4.

Row 8: p4, *sl5 wyib, p7, rep from * to 9 sts from end, sl5 wyib, p4.

Rows 9-10: work in st st.

Row 11: k6, *pick up loose strands and k them tog with next st, k11, rep from * to 7 sts from end, pick up loose strands and k them tog with next st, k6.

Row 12: p6, *sl1 wyif, p11, rep from * to 7 sts from end, sl1 wyif, p6.

Rows 13-18: work in st st.

Row 19 (RS): k10, *sl5 wyif, k7, rep from * to 3 sts from end, k3.

Row 20: p10, *sl5 wyib, p7, rep from * to 3 sts from end, p3.

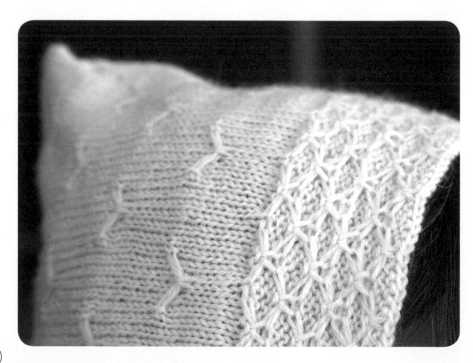

Rows 21-22: work in st st.

Row 23: k12, *pick up loose strands and k them tog with next st, k11, rep from * to last st, k1.

Row 24: p12, *sl1 wyif, p11, rep from * to last st, p1.

Rep rows 1 - 24 for pattern.

ARROW HONEYCOMB
(multiple of 6 sts + 1)

Row 1 (RS): *k1, sl5 wyif; rep from * to last st, k1.

Row 2: *k1, sl5 wyib; rep from * to last st, k1.

Rows 3 and 4: k.

Row 5: *k3, pick up loose strands and k them tog with next st, k2; rep from * to last st, k1.

Row 6: *k3, sl1 wyif, k2; rep from * to last st, k1.

Row 7 (RS): k4, *sl5 wyif, k1; rep from * to 3 sts from end, k3.

Row 8: k4, *sl5 wyib, k1; rep from * to 3 sts from end, k3.

Rows 9 and 10: k.

Row 11: k6, *pick up loose strands and k them tog with next st, k5; rep from * last st, k1.

Row 12: k6, *sl1 wyif, k5; rep from * last st, k1.

Rep rows 1-12 for pattern.

Hood

Hood will be worked back and forth from the centre back out; for the first few rows work half of the stitches and then rearrange so that the already worked half is resting on the cable and the second half can be worked onto the free tip. After a few rows the work will be flexible enough to be worked all at once.

Using figure-of-8 method (see p.4), cast on 178[190, 202]sts, so that there are 89[95, 101]sts on each needle tip. You may find it is neater to use a smaller needle for the cast-on. On the first row, half of the stitches will appear with the right leg towards the back: work into back of these sts to avoid twisting.

Row 1: slide half of cast-on sts onto cable; k89[95, 101]sts from one needle tip, then slide these sts onto cable and slide second set of sts to needle tip and k them. Turn so that WS is facing.

Row 2 (WS) Set-up row: sl1, p1, k5, pm, p21, k1, pm, p to last st on needle tip, pfb, p to last 29 sts, pm, k1, p21, pm, k5, p2.

Row 3: sl1, k1, work row 1 of Arrow Edging patt, slm, k2tog, k to 2 sts before m, kfb, p1, slm, work row 1 of Scattered Arrows patt to m, slm, pfb, k to 2 sts before m, ssk, slm, work row 1 of Arrow Edging patt, k2.

Row 4: sl1, p1, work to m in Arrow Edging patt, slm, p to 1 st before m, k1, slm, work row 2 of Scattered Arrows patt to m, slm, k1, p to m, slm, work Arrow Edging patt over next 5 sts, p2.

Row 5: sl1, k1, work to m in Arrow Edging patt, slm, k2tog, k to 2 sts before m, kfb, p1, slm, work in Scattered Arrows patt to m, slm, pfb, k to 2 sts before m, ssk, slm, work Arrow Edging patt over next 5 sts, k2.

Row 6: sl1, p1, work to m in Arrow Edging patt, slm, p to 1 st before m, k1, slm, work in Scattered Arrows patt to m, slm, k1, p to m, slm, work Arrow Edging patt over next 5 sts, p2.

Rep rows 5 and 6 until work measures approx 6½[7¼, 8]″/16.5[18.5, 20.5] cm from cast-on, ending with row 6 of Arrow edging patt.

Front Edge of hood

Next row (RS): sl1, k1, work to m in Arrow Edging patt, slm, k2tog, k to 2 sts before m, kfb, p1, slm, work in Arrow Honeycomb patt to m, slm, pfb, k to 2 sts before m, ssk, slm, work Arrow Edging patt over next 5 sts, k2.

Next row: sl1, p1, work to m in Arrow Edging patt, slm, p to 1 st before m, k1, slm, work in Arrow Honeycomb patt to m, slm, k1, p to m, slm, work Arrow Edging patt over next 5 sts, p2.

Repeat these two rows 17 more times, ending with row 12 of the Arrow Honeycomb patt.

Separating for scarf ends

Next row (RS): work in patt to 2nd m, remove m, place 29 sts just worked onto holder, bind off 121[133, 145] hood sts to next m, remove m, work in patt to end.

LEFT END OF SCARF (29 STS)

Next row (WS): sl1, p1, work in patt to 2 sts from end, p2.

Next row: sl1, k1, pfb, k to 2 sts before m, ssk, slm, work Arrow Edging patt over 5 sts, k2.

Next row: sl1, p1, work in patt to 2 sts from end, p2.

Rep previous 2 rows until scarf measures approx 9″ / 23cm from hood bind-off ending with row 6 of Arrow Edging patt.

Next row (RS): sl1, k1, work Arrow Honeycomb patt over 25 sts (begin with Row 1), k2.

Next row (WS): sl1, p1, work Arrow Honeycomb patt to last 2 sts, p2.

Work through row 12 of Arrow Honeycomb patt, then work rows 1-6 once more.

Bind off and break yarn.

RIGHT END OF SCARF (29 STS)

Next row (WS): re-join yarn at hood side, work in patt to 2 sts from end, p2.

Next row: sl1, k1, work to m in Arrow edging patt, slm, k2tog, k to 2 sts from end, kfb, k2.

Next row: sl1, p1, work in patt to 2 sts from end, p2.

Rep previous 2 rows until scarf measures approx 9" / 23cm from hood bind-off ending with row 6 of Arrow Edging patt.

Next row (RS): sl1, k1, work Arrow Honeycomb patt over 25 sts (begin with Row 1), k2.

Next row (WS): sl1, p1, work Arrow Honeycomb patt to last 2 sts, p2.

Work through row 12 of Arrow Honeycomb patt once, then work rows 1-6 once.

Bind off and break yarn.

Finishing
Weave in ends and block to measurements.

These socks are named after
one of the yaks at Bijou
Basin Ranch who was very
interested in sniffing them.

Sherman

With this pattern it might finally be time to stop claiming that I'm not a sock knitter. It started with the engineering, a toe-up, heel flap sock with well-fitting arch shaping, that I'd previously tried out with a simple stockinette design. Highlighting the elegance of this shaping with a simple garter rib pattern that flows into cables on the top of the foot and cuffs resulted in something so compelling and fun to knit that I actually completed both socks in the pair myself. It probably helped that the sport weight yarn knits up faster than most sock yarns, plus it results in the slightly heavier socks I covet for wearing inside my winter boots and around the house. They're also pretty good on the yak ranch!

My favourite aspect of the arch shaping is that it creates a bias fabric pointing towards the heel. This means that no short rows are necessary to round the base of the heel before working the "flap" which is worked back and forth, decreasing onto the extra stitches that were added while working the arch shaping.

Materials

Yarn - sport weight yarn: 330 yds / 300 m. Shown in Lorna's Laces Shepherd Sport (100% Superwash Merino Wool, 200yds / 183m, 2.47oz / 70g) in Patina.

Needles - US 2½ / 3mm dpns or long circular(s) for preferred method of working small circumferences in the rnd.

Notions - stitch markers, cable needle.

Gauge

26 sts and 36 rnds = 4″ / 10cm in st st in the rnd.

Sizes

Finished foot circumference, un-stretched, of approx 7″ / 18cm. Sock is very stretchy and will fit foot circumference of 8-9½″ / 20.5-24cm. Length adjustable.

Stitch patterns

Work as follows for first sock; for second sock, change all cables to C4F.

CABLE PATTERN FOR TOP OF FOOT

Rnd 1 (cable rnd): k2, (C4B, k5) twice, C4B, k2.

Rnd 2: (p2, k4, p2, k1) twice, p2, k4, p2.

Rnd 3: k.

Rnd 4: rep rnd 2.

Rnds 5-8: rep rnds 1-4 one more time.

Rnd 9: rep rnd 1 (cable rnd).

Rnds 10-16: rep rnds 2 and 3 three more times, then rnd 2 once.

Rep rnds 1-16 for pattern.

CABLE PATTERN FOR LEG

Rnd 1 (cable rnd): (k2, C4B, k3) to end.

Rnd 2: (p2, k4, p2, k1) to end.

Rnd 3: k.

Rnd 4: (p2, k4, p2, k1) to end.

Rnds 5-8: rep rnds 1-4.

Rnd 9: rep rnd 1 (cable rnd).

Rnds 10-16: rep rnds 2 and 3 three more times, then rnd 2 once.

Rep rnds 1-16 for pattern.

Directions

TOE

Using invisible circular method (see p.4), cast on 9 sts and divide sts evenly for preferred method of knitting small circumferences in the round. K 1 rnd.

Rnd 2: kfb in all sts. 18 sts.

Rnds 3, 5, 7, 9, 11, 13 & 15: k.

Rnd 4: (p1, k1) to end.

Rnd 6: (pfb, k1) to end. 27 sts.

Rnd 8: (p2, k1) to end.

Rnd 10: (p1, m1, p1, k1) to end. 36 sts.

Rnd 12: (p1, k1) to end.

Rnd 14: (pfb, k1) to end. 54 sts.

Rnd 16: (p2, k1) to end.

Arrange sts so that first 26 sts are on needle 1; rem 28 sts are either on cable (magic loop) or needle 2 (two circulars) with a marker in the centre, or divided evenly with 14 sts on needles 2 and 3 (dpns).

FOOT TO CENTRE OF ARCH

Rnd 17: k.

Rnd 18: (p2, k4, p2, k1) twice, p2, k4, p2, (k1, p2) to last st, k1.

Rep rnds 17-18 three more times.

Rnd 25: work sts on needle 1 in cable patt for foot, k1, m1L, k to 3 sts from m at centre of sole, k2tog, k2, ssk, k to 1 st from end, m1R, k1.

Rnd 26: work in patt as set, working increased sts as k or p as required to maintain rib patt.

Rep rnds 25-26 until foot measures approx 4 ¾" / 12cm shorter than desired length from toe to heel, ending with an even rnd that results in full repeats of the rib patt on the sole (i.e. begins k1, p2).

CENTRE OF ARCH TO HEEL

Next rnd: work top of foot sts in patt, k to 2 sts from centre of sole sts, m1R, k4, m1L, k to end.

Next rnd: work in patt as set, working increased sts as k or p as required to maintain rib patt.

Rep last 2 rnds 20 more times, ending with an even rnd that results in full repeats of the rib patt on the sole (i.e. begins k1, p2). 96 sts total, 70 sole sts.

HEEL

Work in patt across top of foot, k to centre of sole sts, k13, ssk, turn.

The heel "flap" will be worked back and forth, ignore top of foot sts until heel is complete.

Next row: sl1, (k2, p1) 8 times, k2, p2tog, turn.

Next row: sl1, k to slipped st, ssk, turn.

Next row: sl1, work in rib patt to slipped st, p2tog, turn.

Rep last 2 rows 18 more times,
until 1 sole st on each side remains
unincorporated.

Next row: sl1, k to slipped st, ssk, do
not turn.

LEG

Next rnd: work top of foot sts in patt
as set, k2tog, (p2, k4, p2, k1) to end.

Work in cable patt for leg, beg with
rnd to follow last rnd of top of foot
patt, until leg measures approx 1" /
2.5cm less than desired length, ending
with rnd 8 or 16.

CUFF

Next rnd: k.

Next rnd: (p2, k1) to end.

Rep last 2 rnds 6 more times.

Bind off with a loose, stretchy method.

FINISHING
Weave in ends and block.

Sherilyn

A few years ago I was obsessed with creating illustrative lace patterns, most of which ended up simply looking messy. It turns out that there are good reasons that most traditional lace patterns are simple, geometric representations of things like leaves and feathers. A stylized representation of a pair of cherries on their stalks turned out rather successfully and the pattern flowed well into columns of a simple geometric mesh pattern. And so I knit a shawl, but my design abilities were rather ahead of my pattern creation abilities and it took a little while to catch up in addition to simply finding the time to revisit the idea but I'm so glad to finally be sharing it.

The triangular shawl is shown in two sizes, either of which can be knit in lace or fingering weight, and is flexible enough to be made as large as you wish.

Materials

Yarn - fingering / 4ply or lace weight yarn: 430[510]yds / 395[470]m.

Larger shawl shown in Cephalopod Yarns Skinny Bugga (80% superwash merino, 10% cashmere, 10% nylon, 450yds / 411m, 3.99oz / 113g) in Rose Weevil.

Smaller shawl shown in Jade Sapphire Mongolian Cashmere 2ply (100% cashmere, 400yds / 366m, 1.84oz / 55g) in Cousin Coral.

Needles - US 5 / 3.75mm 32" / 80cm or longer circular.

Gauge

16 sts and 28 rows = 4" / 10cm in mesh pattern, well blocked.

23 sts and 35 rows = 4" / 10cm in st st.

Sizes

Upper edge: approx 48[58]" / 122[147]cm; centre length: 24[29]" / 61[74]cm.

Pam's cute dress is her
Rally pattern from the book
Knitting it Old School.

Directions

Using figure-of-8 method (see page 4), cast on 6 sts - 3 on each needle tip. Work first few rows back and forth across all sts, keeping half of the sts on the needle cord at a time (as though doing magic loop). After a few rows there will be enough fabric to simply work across the whole row.

Work shawl from either written directions or charts (p. 70). Work section one once, section two 2[3] times (can be repeated as many times as desired to make a larger shawl), section three once, ending with section four once.

Written directions

WS ROWS - *work all WS rows by alternating the following 2 rows:*

WS row 1: k2, p1, k1, p to 2 sts from end, k1, yo2, k1.

WS row 2: bind off 2, k2, p to 4 sts from end, k4.

To check which row to work next, look at the work - if a double yarn over was worked on the edging at the end of the previous RS row, work WS row 1.

SECTION 1
Work once.

Row 1 (RS): k3, yo, k2, yo2, k1. 9 sts.

Row 3: k1, p1, k3, k1tbl, k5. 11 sts.

In following rows, the instructions between asterisks are for the side panels and are worked twice separated by the centre spine stitch. On the chart, the second repetition is indicated by the marked column and is not shown.

Refer to table on page 69 for st counts in each side panel after every row.

Row 5: bind off 2 sts, k2, *yo, k1tbl, yo*, k1tbl, rep from * to * once more, k1, yo2, k1.

Row 7: k1, p1, k2, *yo, k3, yo*, k1tbl, rep from * to * once more, k4.

Row 9: bind off 2 sts, k2, *yo, k1tbl, yo, sl1, k2tog, psso, yo, k1tbl, yo*, k1tbl, rep from * to * once more, k1, yo2, k1.

Row 11: k1, p1, k2, *yo, k2tog, yo, k3, yo, ssk, yo*, k1tbl, rep from * to * once more, k4.

Row 13: bind off 2 sts, k2, *yo, k3, yo, sl1, k2tog, psso, yo, k3, yo*, k1tbl, rep from * to * once more, k1, yo2, k1.

Row 15: k1, p1, k2, *yo, k1tbl, yo, sl1, k2tog, psso, yo, k3, yo, sl1, k2tog, psso, yo, k1tbl, yo*, k1tbl, rep from * to * once more, k4.

Row 17: bind off 2 sts, k2, *yo, k2tog, yo, k3, yo, sl1, k2tog, psso, yo, k3, yo, ssk, yo*, k1tbl, rep from * to * once more, k1, yo2, k1.

Row 19: k1, p1, k2, *yo, (k3, yo, sl1, k2tog, psso, yo) twice, k3, yo*, k1tbl, rep from * to * once more, k4.

Row 21: bind off 2 sts, k2, *yo, k1tbl, (yo, sl1, k2tog, psso, yo, k3) twice, yo, sl1, k2tog, psso, yo, k1tbl, yo*, k1tbl, rep from * to * once more, k1, yo2, k1.

Complete section 1 with WS row 1.

SECTION 2
Work 2[3] times.

Row 1: k1, p1, k2, *yo, **k5, (yo, sl1, k2tog, psso, yo, k3) twice, k1, rep from ** to 1 st from end of side panel section, k1, yo*, k1tbl, rep from * to * once more, k4.

Row 3: bind off 2 sts, k2, *yo, **k3, yo, sl1, k2tog, psso, yo, rep from ** to 3 sts from end of side panel section, k3, yo*, k1tbl, rep from * to * once more, k1, yo2, k1.

Row 5: k1, p1, k2, *yo, k2, **k5, (yo, sl1, k2tog, psso, yo, k3) twice, k1, rep from ** to 3 sts from end of side panel section, k3, yo*, k1tbl, rep from * to * once more, k4.

Row 7: bind off 2 sts, k2, *yo, k2tog, yo, **k3, yo, sl1, k2tog, psso, yo, rep from ** to 5 sts from end of side panel section, k3, yo, ssk, yo*, k1tbl, rep from * to * once more, k1, yo2, k1.

SECTION 2, CONTINUED

Row 9: k1, p1, k2, *yo, k4, **k5, (yo, sl1, k2tog, psso, yo, k3) twice, k1, rep from ** to 5 sts from the end of side panel section, k5, yo*, k1tbl, rep from * to * once more, k4.

Row 11: bind off 2 sts, k2, *yo, k1tbl, **yo, sl1, k2tog, psso, yo, k3, rep from ** to 4 sts from end of side panel section, yo, sl1, k2tog, psso, yo, k1tbl, yo*, k1tbl, rep from * to * once more, k1, yo2, k1.

Row 13: k1, p1, k2, *yo, k2tog, yo, k4, ** k5, (yo, sl1, k2tog, psso, yo, k3) twice, k1, rep from ** to 7 sts from end of side panel section, k5, yo, ssk, yo*, k1tbl, rep from * to * once more, k4.

Row 15: bind off 2 sts, k2, *yo, **k3, yo, sl1, k2tog, psso, yo, rep from ** to 3 sts from end of side panel section, k3, yo*, k1tbl, rep from * to * once more, k1, yo2, k1.

Row 17: k1, p1, k2, *yo, k1tbl, yo, sl1, k2tog, psso, yo, k4, **k5, (yo, sl1, k2tog, psso, yo, k3) twice, k1, rep from ** to 9 sts from end of side panel section, k5, yo, sl1, k2tog, psso, yo, k1tbl, yo*, k1tbl, rep from * to * once more, k4.

Row 19: bind off 2 sts, k2, *yo, k2tog, yo, **k3, yo, sl1, k2tog, psso, yo, rep from ** to 5 sts from end of side panel section, k3, yo, ssk, yo*, k1tbl, rep from * to * once more, k1, yo2, k1.

Row 21: k1, p1, k2, *yo, k3, **yo, sl1, k2tog, psso, yo, k9, yo, sl1, k2tog, psso, yo, k3, rep from ** to end of side panel section, yo*, k1tbl, rep from * to * once more, k4.

Row 23: bind off 2 sts, k2, *yo, k1tbl, yo, sl1, k2tog, psso, yo, **k3, yo, sl1, k2tog, psso, yo, rep from ** to 1 st from end of side panel section, k1tbl, yo*, k1tbl, rep from * to * once more, k1, yo2, k1.

Row 25: k1, p1, k2, *yo, k2tog, yo, k3, **yo, sl1, k2tog, psso, yo, k9, yo, sl1, k2tog, psso, yo, k3, rep from ** to 2 sts from end of side panel section, yo, ssk, yo*, k1tbl, rep from * to * once more, k4.

Row 27: bind off 2 sts, k2, *yo, **k3, yo, sl1, k2tog, psso, yo, rep from ** to 3 sts from end of side panel section, k3, yo*, k1tbl, rep from * to * once more, k1, yo2, k1.

Row 29: k1, p1, k2, *yo, k1tbl, yo, sl1, k2tog, psso, yo, k3, yo, sl1, k2tog, psso, yo, **k9, yo, sl1, k2tog, psso, yo, k3, yo, sl1, k2tog, psso, yo, rep from ** to 1 st from end of side panel section, k1tbl, yo*, k1tbl, rep from * to * once more, k4.

Row 31: bind off 2 sts, k2, *yo, k2tog, yo, **k3, yo, sl1, k2tog, psso, yo, rep from ** to 5 sts from end of side panel section, k3, yo, ssk, yo*, k1tbl, rep from * to * once more, k1, yo2, k1.

Row 33: k1, p1, k2, *yo, k3, yo, sl1, k2tog, psso, yo, k3, yo, sl1, k2tog, psso, yo, **k9, yo, sl1, k2tog, psso, yo, k3, yo, sl1, k2tog, psso, yo, rep from ** to 3 sts from end of side panel section, k3, yo*, k1tbl, rep from * to * once more, k4.

Row 35: bind off 2 sts, k2, *yo, k1tbl, yo, sl1, k2tog, psso, yo, **k3, yo, sl1, k2tog, psso, yo, rep from ** to 1 st from end of side panel section, k1tbl, yo*, k1tbl, rep from * to * once more, k1, yo2, k1.

Complete section 2 with WS row 1.

SECTION 3
Work once.

Row 1: k1, p1, k2, *yo, **k1tbl, yo, (ssk, yo) twice, sl1, k2tog, psso, yo, k3, yo, sl1, k2tog, psso, (yo, k2tog) twice, yo, rep from ** to 1 st from end of side panel section, k1tbl, yo*, k1tbl, rep from * to * once more, k4.

Row 3: bind off 2 sts, k2, *yo, k1, **k2, yo, (ssk, yo) 3 times, sl1, k2tog, psso, (yo, k2tog) 3 times, yo, k1, rep from ** to 2 sts from end of side panel section, k2, yo*, k1tbl, rep from * to * once more, k1, yo2, k1.

Row 5: k1, p1, k2, *yo, k2tog, yo, **k1tbl, (yo, ssk) 4 times, k1, (k2tog, yo) 4 times, rep from ** to 3 sts from end of side panel section, k1tbl, yo, ssk, yo*, k1tbl, rep from * to * once more, k4.

Row 7: bind off 2 sts, k2, *yo, k2tog, yo, k1 **k2, (yo, ssk) 3 times, yo, sl1, k2tog, psso, yo, (k2tog, yo) 3 times, k1, rep from ** to 4 sts from end of side panel section, k2, yo, ssk, yo*, k1tbl, rep from * to * once more, k1, yo2, k1.

Row 9: k1, p1, k2, *yo, k2tog, yo, k2, **k3, (yo, ssk) 3 times, k1, (k2tog, yo) 3 times, k2, rep from ** to 5 sts from end of side panel section, k3, yo, ssk, yo*, k1tbl, work * to * once, k4.

Row 11: bind off 2 sts, k2, *yo, k2, yo, ssk, k1, **k2, k2tog, yo, k2, yo, ssk, yo, sl1, k2tog, psso, yo, k2tog, yo, k2, yo, ssk, k1, rep from ** to 6 sts from end of side panel section, k2, k2tog, yo, k2, yo*, k1tbl, work * to * once, k1, yo2, k1.

Row 13: k1, p1, k2, *yo, k4, yo, ssk, **k1, k2tog, yo, k4, yo, ssk, k1, k2tog, yo, k4, yo, ssk, rep from ** to 7 sts from end of side panel section, k1, k2tog, yo, k4, yo*, k1tbl, work * to * once, k4.

Row 15: bind off 2 sts, k2, *yo, k6, yo, **sl1, k2tog, psso, yo, k6, yo, rep from ** to end of side panel section*, k1tbl, rep from * to * once more, k1, yo2, k1.

Row 17: k1, p1, k2, *yo, k1tbl, yo, k6, yo, **sl1, k2tog, psso, yo, k6, yo, k3, yo, k6, yo, rep from ** to 10 sts from end of side panel section, sl1, k2tog, psso, yo, k6, yo, k1tbl, yo*, k1tbl, rep from * to * once more, k4.

Row 19: bind off 2 sts, k2, *yo, k1, k2tog, yo, k6, yo, **sl1, k2tog, psso, yo, k6, k5, yo, k6, yo, rep from ** to 12 sts from end of side panel section, sl1, k2tog, psso, yo, k6, yo, ssk, k1, yo*, k1tbl, rep from * to * once more, k1, yo2, k1.

Row 21: k1, p1, k2, *yo, k1, k2tog, yo, k1tbl, yo, ssk, k2, k2tog, yo, **sl1, k2tog, psso, yo, ssk, k2, k2tog, yo, k1tbl, yo, ssk, k1, k2tog, yo, k1tbl, yo, ssk, k2, k2tog, yo, rep from ** to 13 sts from end of side panel section, sl1, k2tog, psso, yo, ssk, k2, k2tog, yo, k1tbl, yo, ssk, k1, yo*, k1tbl, rep from * to * once more, k4.

Row 23: bind off 2 sts, k2, *yo, sl1, k2tog, psso, yo, k3, yo, sl1, k3tog, psso, yo, k1, **k2, yo, sl1, k3tog, psso, yo, k3, yo, sl1, k2tog, psso, yo, k3, yo, sl1, k3tog, psso, yo, k1, rep from ** to 12 sts from end of side panel section k2, yo, sl1, k3tog, psso, yo, k3, yo, sl1, k2tog, psso, yo*, k1tbl, work * to * once, k1, yo2, k1.

Row 25: k1, p1, k2, *yo, k2tog, yo, k4, (k2tog, yo) twice, **k1tbl, (yo, ssk) twice, k4, yo, k1tbl, yo, k4, (k2tog, yo) twice, rep from ** to 11 sts from end of side panel section, k1tbl, (yo, ssk) twice, k4, yo, ssk, yo*, k1tbl, rep from * to * once more, k4.

Row 27: bind off 2 sts, k2, *yo, k2tog, yo, k1tbl, yo, ssk, k1, (k2tog, yo) twice, k1, **k2, (yo, ssk) twice, k1, k2tog, yo, sl1, k2tog, psso, yo, ssk, k1, (k2tog, yo) twice, k1, rep from ** to 12 sts from end of side panel section, k2, (yo, ssk) twice, k1, k2tog, yo, k1tbl, yo, ssk, yo*, k1tbl, rep from * to * once more, k1, yo2, k1.

Row 29: k1, p1, k2, *yo, k2tog, yo, k3, yo, sl1, k2tog, psso, yo, k2tog, yo, k2, **k3, yo, ssk, yo, sl1, k2tog, psso, yo, k3, yo, sl1, k2tog, psso, yo, k2tog, yo, k2) rep from ** to 13 sts from end of side panel section, k3, yo, ssk, yo, sl1, k2tog, psso, yo, k3, yo, ssk, yo*, k1tbl, rep from * to * once more, k4.

Row 31: bind off 2 sts, k2, *yo, k2, yo, k4, k2tog, yo, k2, yo, ssk, k1, **k2, k2tog, yo, k2, yo, ssk, k3, k2tog, yo, k2, yo, ssk, k1, rep from ** to 14 sts from end of side panel section, k2, k2tog, yo, k2, yo, ssk, k4, yo, k2, yo*, k1tbl, rep from * to * once more, k1, yo2, k1.

Row 33: k1, p1, k2, *yo, k4, yo, ssk, k1, k2tog, yo, k4, yo, ssk, **k1, k2tog, yo, k4, yo, ssk, k1, k2tog, yo, k4, yo, ssk, rep from ** to 16 sts from end of side panel section, k1, k2tog, yo, k4, yo, ssk, k1, k2tog, yo, k4, yo*, k1tbl, rep from * to * once more, k4.

Row 35: bind off 2 sts, k2, *yo, **k6, yo, sl1, k2tog, psso, yo, rep from ** to 6 sts from end of side panel section, k6, yo*, k1tbl, rep from * to * once more, k1, yo2, k1.

Row 37: k1, p1, k2, *yo, k1tbl, yo, k6, yo, k3, yo, k6, yo, **sl1, k2tog, psso, yo, k6, yo, k3, yo, k6, yo, rep from ** to 1 st from end of side panel section, k1tbl, yo*, k1tbl, rep from * to * once more, k4.

Row 39: bind off 2 sts, k2, *yo, **sl1, k2tog, psso, yo, k6, yo, k5, yo, k6, yo rep from ** to 3 sts from end of side panel section, sl1, k2tog, psso, yo*, k1tbl, work * to * once, k1, yo2, k1.

Row 41: k1, p1, k2, *yo, **sl1, k2tog, psso, yo, ssk, k2, k2tog, yo, k1tbl, yo, ssk, k1, k2tog, yo, k1tbl, yo, ssk, k2, k2tog, yo, rep from ** to 3 sts from end of side panel section, sl1, k2tog, psso, yo*, k1tbl, rep from * to * once more, k4.

Row 43: bind off 2 sts, k2, *yo, k1, **k2, yo, sl1, k3tog, psso, yo, k3, yo, sl1, k2tog, psso, yo, k3, yo, sl1, k3tog, psso, yo, k1, rep from ** to 2 sts from end of side panel, k2, yo*, k1tbl, work * to * once, k1, yo2, k1.

Complete section 3 with WS row 1.

SECTION 4
Work once.

Row 1: k1, p1, k2, yo, k5, *yo, k1, yo, k5, rep from * to 4 sts from end, yo, k4.

Row 3: bind off 2 sts, k2, yo, k2, sl1, k2tog, psso, k2, *yo, k1, yo, k2, sl1, k2tog, psso, k2, rep from * to 2 sts from end, yo, k1, yo2, k1.

Complete section 4 with WS row 1.

Finishing

Bind off loosely from RS.

Weave in ends. Wet block, pinning top edge straight and pinning out eyelets along bottom edge into points.

Clara Parkes: "a good skein of cashmere makes everything better."

Sts in each side panel section

Section 1

Row	St count
1	1
3	1
5	3
7	5
9	7
11	9
13	11
15	13
17	15
19	17
21	19

Section 2

Row	St count		
	1st rep	2nd rep	3rd rep
1	21	57	93
3	23	59	95
5	25	61	97
7	27	63	99
9	29	65	101
11	31	67	103
13	33	69	105
15	35	71	107
17	37	73	109
19	39	75	111
21	41	77	113
23	43	79	115
25	45	81	117
27	47	83	119
29	49	85	121
31	51	87	123
33	53	89	125
35	55	91	127

Section 3

Row	St count	
	after 2 reps section 2	after 3 reps section 2
1	93	129
3	95	131
5	97	133
7	99	135
9	101	137
11	103	139
13	105	141
15	107	143
17	117	157
19	125	169
21	119	159
23	111	147
25	119	159
27	115	151
29	117	153
31	121	157
33	123	159
35	125	161
37	139	179
39	149	193
41	139	179
43	131	167

Chart, section 1 - work once

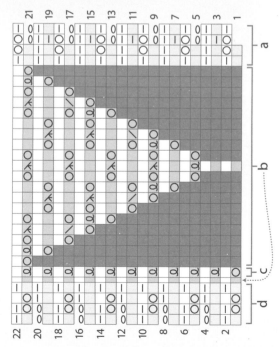

Chart Notes

a. Right edging: work once

b. Side panel, worked on each side of centre spine: work once, then work centre spine st and repeat side panel once more

c. Centre spine stitch

d. Left edging: work once

Chart Key

- ☐ k on rs, p on ws
- ⊟ p on rs, k on ws
- Ⓞ yo
- Ⓠ k1tbl

- ⋏ sl1, k2tog, psso
- ∕ k2tog
- ∖ ssk
- ○ bind off 1 st

- ▨ no stitch
- ☐ repeat the stitches inside this box

Chart, section 2 - work full 36-row sequence 2[3] times

Chart, section 3 - work once

Chart, section 4 - work once

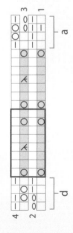

Chart Key

- ☐ k on rs, p on ws
- ⊟ p on rs, k on ws
- O yo
- ⬚ k1 tbl
- ⟁ sl1, k2tog, psso
- ⟰ sl1 k3tog, psso
- ⟋ k2tog
- ⟍ ssk
- o bind off 1 st
- ▦ no stitch
- ☐ repeat the stitches inside this box

Chart Notes

a. Right edging: work once

b. Side panel, worked on each side of centre spine: work once, then work centre spine st and repeat side panel once more

c. Centre spine stitch

d. Left edging: work once

Book design

Julie Levesque   www.symposi.com

Models

Thank you to all of the dear, and wonderfully creative, friends who responded eagerly when I asked them to don some knitwear and let me take photographs of them.

Sarah Bible   www.onestitchshort.com

Mary-Heather Cogar   www.rainydaygoods.com

Amber Corcoran   www.fancytiger.com/craftindex.html
& Jaime Jennings

Erica Marshall   www.ravelry.com/people/erica

Melissa LaBarre   www.knittingschooldropout.com

Clara Parkes   www.knittersreview.com

Pamela Wynne   www.flintknits.com

Stephen West   www.westknits.com

And of course, the adorable babies who kept sneaking into my photos even when they weren't supposed to, Carson and Eloise.

Technical Editing

Kristi Porter   www.domesticsphere.com

Additional editing by

Alison Green Will   www.alisongreenwill.com

Laura Chau   www.cosmicpluto.com

other designs by Ysolda

eBook

Carefully scratch off the silver panel
opposite to reveal a unique code.
To download your complimentary
digital version of this book enter the
code at www.ysolda.com/redeem

scratch off with a coin →